A Water Report
Natural Water

Michael and Jane Pelusey

MACMILLAN
LIBRARY

First published in 2006 by
MACMILLAN EDUCATION AUSTRALIA PTY LTD
627 Chapel Street, South Yarra 3141

Visit our website at www.macmillan.com.au

Associated companies and representatives throughout the world.

National Library of Australia
Cataloguing-in-Publication data

Pelusey, Michael.
    Natural water.

    Includes index.
    For middle and upper primary aged children.
    ISBN 9 78142020 3080.

    ISBN 1 42020308 8.

    1. Water - Juvenile literature. I. Pelusey, Jane. II.
    Title. (Series : Pelusey, Michael. Water report).

    553.7

Edited by Sally Green
Text and cover design by Cristina Neri, Canary Graphic Design
Page layout by Cristina Neri, Canary Graphic Design
Maps by Alan Laver, Shelly Communications Pty Ltd

Printed in China

Acknowledgements
Michael and Jane would like to thank Water Corporation of Western Australia.

Cover photographs: creek in the highlands of Tasmania (front); a lake in Tasmania's
mountains (back).

All photographs © Pelusey Photography.

Contents

GLOSSARY WORDS
When a word is printed in **bold**,
you can look up its meaning in the
Glossary on page 31.

Water

Water is essential for life. Without water there would be no plants, animals or humans on the planet. Water on Earth formed billions of years ago, so water coming out of our taps is nearly as old as the planet itself.

At room temperature, water is a liquid. When the water temperature drops below zero degrees Celsius, it freezes into a solid called ice. When water is heated, it **evaporates** and turns into a gas called **water vapour**.

Water is a limited resource, but the number of people using it is growing. It is vital we look after our water resources.

Water as a liquid

Water as ice

Waterwise Fact

Our bodies are made of 70 per cent water.

Every cell in our body contains water. We lose water through sweat, our breath and urine. We need to replace that amount of water every day by drinking.

Water as a vapour

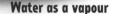

4

Natural water

Natural water can be fresh water or salt water. It exists in oceans, rivers, lakes and swamps. Some natural water seeps through soil and rock and collects underground. This water is called **ground water**.

Most of the world's water is salt water. In fact, about 70 per cent of the Earth is covered by oceans of salt water. Fresh water only makes up a small part of the total amount of water on Earth. Living things need fresh water to survive.

Natural water is essential to the health of our planet. It is in the Earth's **atmosphere**, on the ground and under the ground. It is all around us.

Yellow Water, Northern Territory

Fresh water in a creek in the highlands of Tasmania

Waterwise Fact

How salty is the sea?

For every 1000 kilograms of sea water there is 35 kilograms of salt. Fresh water has only the tiniest trace of salt—so little that we cannot taste it.

Sea water in Encounter Bay, South Australia

The water cycle

Water is constantly changing from water vapour into liquid water and back to water vapour. This constant system of change is called the water cycle. There is no beginning to the cycle and there is no end. No new water enters the cycle, and no used water leaves it.

The Sun
The Sun heats the world's seas, rivers and lakes. Even small puddles are heated by the Sun.

Precipitation

Heating

Further condensation

As the white clouds rise, they cool further. The small, fine water droplets join to become bigger water droplets, making the clouds heavier and darker. Eventually the clouds are so heavy with water they fall as rain, hail or snow.

Further condensation

Condensation

Small, fine water droplets join together to form fluffy, white clouds.

Precipitation

The rain, hail or snow, called **precipitation**, falls on land. The **run-off** from rainwater, melted ice and snow flows into lakes and rivers and out to the sea. In some places water soaks into the ground and collects in **aquifers**.

Water vapour

Evaporation

Heated water in seas, rivers and lakes evaporates and turns into a gas, called water vapour.

Water vapour

As the water vapour rises, it cools to form water droplets. This is called **condensation**.

Fresh water

Only a very, very small amount of the world's water is fresh water. The rest is salty and not suitable for plants, animals and people to use. A lot of the world's fresh water is in the form of ice, so it cannot be used. Most of this ice is in the icecaps of the Arctic and the Antarctic, in icebergs and in **glaciers**.

Some of the fresh water that is not frozen is in places that are too hard to reach, such as in high and rugged mountains.

This lake high up in Tasmania's mountains contains fresh water, but it is too far from towns for people to use the water.

Much of the world's fresh water is frozen and locked up in glaciers.

8

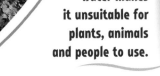
The salt in sea water makes it unsuitable for plants, animals and people to use.

Availability of fresh water

Most fresh water collects in places where people cannot use it, such as oceans or huge mountains. Only 0.08 per cent of the world's water is available for people to use worldwide. This is the same amount of water that was available to people living thousands of years ago. Today there are many more people needing to use the same small amount of water.

Waterwise Fact

How much water?

Amount of water	Cubic kilometres
On Earth	1 385 000 000
Total fresh water on the Earth	37 300 000
Fresh water frozen in icecaps and glaciers	4 710 000
Water held in the atmosphere as water vapour	13 500
Ground water	8 450 000
Water in rivers	1 500

Growing Australian cities are using more and more water.

Waterways

Both salt water and fresh water collect in areas that are called waterways. Waterways are very important for supplying water to people and wildlife. Waterways include oceans, seas, rivers, lakes and **wetlands**.

Oceans and seas

Oceans and seas are large bodies of salt water that surround land. The continent of Australia is surrounded by oceans and seas. Most water vapour in the atmosphere comes from evaporation of oceans and seas. Wind blows the water vapour towards land, where it rises and forms rain clouds.

Waterwise Fact

Australia's ocean currents

Australia's west coast receives more rainfall than the west coasts of other continents because of the warm Leeuwin Current. Other west coasts have cold currents.

Warm, moving streams of water in oceans, called warm currents, produce more water vapour than cold currents. Therefore they produce more rain. Land which has a warm current near it has a greater rainfall.

Lord Howe Island, off the New South Wales coast, has high rainfall due to the warm east Australian current which flows nearby.

The Murray River meets the Darling River at Wentworth, New South Wales, to become the Murray–Darling River.

Rivers

Rivers are another type of waterway. A river begins life as a small stream. Streams get their water from rainfall or melting ice in high, hilly or mountainous regions. Small streams join with other streams or **tributaries** to form a river. Rivers carry a lot of water to a larger body of water, such as an ocean or a lake.

Although many rivers flow throughout the year in Australia, some do not. In inland Australia, some rivers may stay dry for many years if it does not rain. Some inland rivers only flow occasionally, after heavy rain.

Waterwise Fact

Australia's longest river

The Murray–Darling River is the longest river system in Australia. It flows through three states, New South Wales, Victoria and South Australia, and is half as long as the Nile River in Africa.

Major Rivers of Australia	
State	**Rivers**
Queensland	Flinders, Tully, Brisbane, Burdekin
New South Wales	Darling, Murray, Snowy, Murrumbidgee, Lachlan, Barwon, Macintyre
Australian Capital Territory	Murrumbidgee, Queanbeyan
Victoria	Goulburn, Murray, Yarra
Tasmania	South Esk, Derwent, Gordon, Franklin
South Australia	Murray, Cooper Creek, Torrens
Western Australia	Gascoyne, Fitzroy, Ord, Blackwood, Swan, Warren, Murchison, Drysdale
Northern Territory	Daly, South Alligator, Katherine, Victoria, Todd

Lake Lefroy's salt water has evaporated, turning it into a dry salt lake.

Lakes

Lakes are waterways that are surrounded by land. Lakes form where water flows from higher ground down to natural basins. Most lakes near the coast of Australia get run-off from regular rainfall and remain full all year. In drier, inland parts of Australia, lakes rapidly dry up due to high evaporation. They are called salt lakes because when the water evaporates, salt is left behind. Very little wildlife can live near salt lakes as there is not enough fresh water available.

Lakes also form in ancient volcano craters. Blue Lake, at Mount Gambier in South Australia, is a crater lake. Some lakes in mountainous regions were formed by the movement of glaciers that hollowed out the hard rock many thousands of years ago.

Artificial lakes are sometimes created when rivers are dammed.

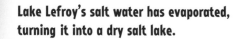

Waterwise Fact

Australia's largest lake

Lake Eyre in South Australia is 9300 square kilometres in area. Most of the time it is a dry salt lake. In the last 150 years Lake Eyre has been nearly full only three times.

Major Lakes of Australia	
State	**Lakes**
Queensland	Lake Dalrymple, Lake Wivenhoe
New South Wales	Lake Garnpung, Lake Eucumbene, Minindee Lakes
Australian Capital Territory	Lake Burley Griffin
Victoria	Lake Corangamite, Lake Wellington, Lake Tyrell
Tasmania	Lake Gordon, Lake Pedder, Dove Lake, Lake St Clair
South Australia	Lake Eyre, Lake Torrens, Lake Frome, Lake Gairdner
Western Australia	Lake Jasper, Lake Argyle, Lake Lefroy, Lake Leschenaultia
Northern Territory	Lake Amadeus, Lake de Burgh

Issues affecting waterways

The two main issues affecting waterways are water pollution and **algal blooms**. Animals and plants need clean water in waterways to thrive. Water pollution, **sewage** and algal blooms make the water in waterways dirty and unusable.

Water pollution

Water pollution is caused by chemicals and other harmful substances, such as fertilisers, that enter the water. Chemicals dumped into waterways poison the water, killing water creatures and making the water unfit to drink. Sewage from leaking pipes can find its way through drains into rivers. Sewage is full of harmful bacteria that cause disease.

Governments have strict rules to keep water pollution to a minimum. Companies are not allowed to dump chemical waste in waterways, and sewage water must be cleaned before it enters a waterway. Natural water can remain clean if pollution and chemicals do not enter waterways.

This fish was killed by pollution that entered the waterway further upstream.

Algal blooms

Algae are tiny plants that live in the water. They feed on any fertiliser that may enter the water, and grow into a slime called an algal bloom. This slime covers the surface of the water and stops oxygen from entering the water. The plant and animal life living in the waterway die without oxygen.

When an algal bloom dies and breaks down, its toxins can be harmful to people.

Water Saver Tip

Protect local waterways

Schools and communities can help keep their local waterways healthy by working with organisations, such as Waterwatch.

Ground water

Ground water is natural water that is found underground. It is a very important source of fresh water. Ground water is the most common form of fresh water in the world, except for the frozen icecaps. Nearly all unfrozen fresh water is found underground.

Most people who live in country areas around the world rely on ground water for all their water supply. Australia has reserves of ground water which are used by farmers. Windmills pump water to the surface. Even some cities in Australia use ground water as a major source of drinking water.

Windmills are used to pump ground water to the surface to water crops.

A man bathes in ground water from a village well in Vietnam.

Waterwise Fact

Ground water supply

Around the world, 1.5 billion people rely on ground water for their water supply.

Aquifers

Ground water is mostly found in aquifers. When it rains, some water runs off into waterways and some soaks through the soil. The water that soaks through areas of **porous** material, such as limestone, sandstone and sand, collects underground in aquifers. There are two types of aquifers:

- artesian basins, known as confined aquifers
- unconfined aquifers.

Artesian basins are formed when ground water becomes trapped in porous material between two layers of solid rock. Pressure builds up between the two layers. When a **bore** is drilled into a confined aquifer, the pressure is released, sending water to the surface without pumping.

Artesian basins sometimes form deep within the Earth where it is hot. When this artesian water reaches the surface it often needs to be cooled before it can be used.

Unconfined aquifers usually form closer to the Earth's surface than artesian basins. This type of water sits above a layer of rock and is not under pressure.

The upper level of an aquifer is called the water table. Water collects in an aquifer under the water table and above the layer of rock.

Waterwise Fact

Water in aquifers

Water in aquifers flows slowly towards the sea, moving only a few centimetres a year.

Ground water in Australia

Most of Australia's ground water contains dissolved salts and minerals. This makes it unsuitable for humans to drink. However, cattle and sheep can drink it, and it can be used to water crops.

The biggest artesian basins in Australia are:

- Great Artesian Basin (in Queensland, New South Wales, South Australia, Northern Territory)
- Canning Basin (in Western Australia)
- Daly–Georgina Basin (in Northern Territory and Queensland)
- Murray–Darling Basin (in Victoria and South Australia)
- Yarragadee Aquifer (in Western Australia).

There are small, unconfined aquifers in various parts of Australia. Some unconfined aquifers are so close to the surface that they form lakes. These lakes provide a home for many waterbirds, frogs and other water animals.

Waterwise Fact

Biggest supply of ground water

The Great Artesian Basin has the biggest supply of ground water in the world. It covers an area of 1.7 million square kilometres in Queensland, parts of New South Wales, South Australia and the Northern Territory. It holds 8700 megalitres of water.

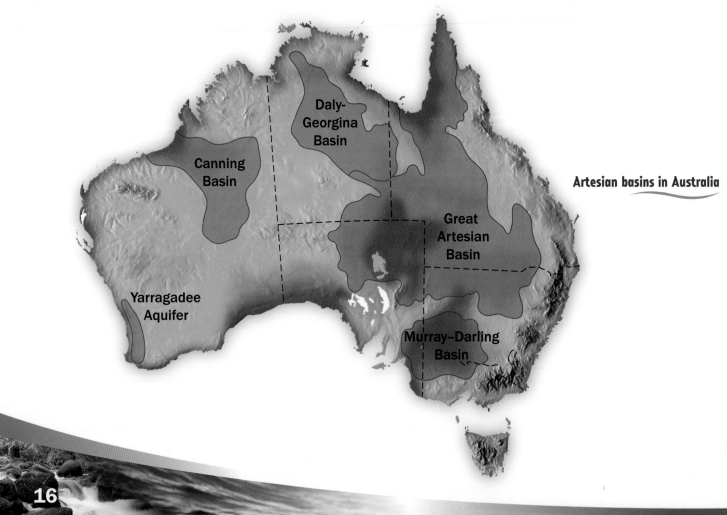

Artesian basins in Australia

Issues affecting ground water

The two main issues affecting the amount of ground water we have to use are pollution and overuse.

Pollution

Chemicals such as fertilisers, pesticides and **industrial waste** seep through soil and pollute ground water. The pollutants contaminate good-quality ground water, making it less suitable for drinking. Proper sewage treatment and environmental controls help prevent pollution.

Overuse

Ground water is the main supply of water in some parts of Australia. The water table in aquifers may drop if too much ground water is taken from the aquifers. As a result, the roots of trees and plants cannot reach the water table, causing them to die. Surface lakes and wetlands linked to the aquifers are drying up in some places because so much water has been taken from the aquifers.

Another problem is that less water from rainfall is reaching ground water aquifers because of Australia's drying climate. This means that ground water is being used more quickly than it can be replaced.

In 1987, Perry Lakes in Perth had plenty of water.

Waterwise Fact
The Great Artesian Basin

The Great Artesian Basin has bores that do not turn off. They flow 24 hours a day, providing water for animals. Now they are having taps put on them to save water.

In 2005, Perry Lakes was dry most of the year.

Climate and water

The climate affects the amount of natural water in any particular area. Climate is the pattern of weather in a region over a period of years. The Sun's heat has the most impact on climate. The Earth's climate is warmest near the equator where the Sun's rays are at their most direct.

Further from the equator land heats up and cools down unevenly. Ocean temperatures change less than temperatures on land. These differences in temperature create air masses that move around, producing our weather patterns.

The weather pattern in a region will affect the amount of rainfall that a region gets. Australia has six major climate types or zones, each with its own rainfall and temperature patterns.

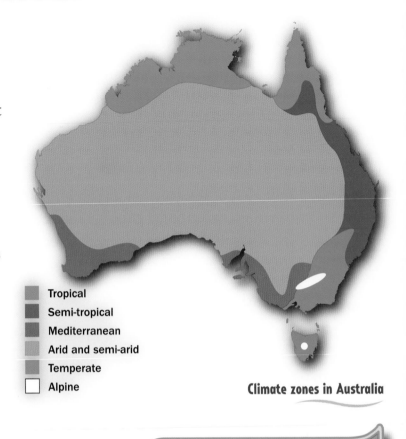

- Tropical
- Semi-tropical
- Mediterranean
- Arid and semi-arid
- Temperate
- Alpine

Climate zones in Australia

More rain generally falls in mountainous regions.

Waterwise Fact

Evaporation rates

Evaporation is affected by four things:
- water temperature
- air humidity (the amount of water vapour in the air)
- air pressure
- wind speed.

18

Tropical wet and dry climate

Northern Australia experiences a wet and dry climate. Warm, moist air blows in from the sea and produces very heavy rain and thunderstorms during the hot and humid wet season. Rivers and lakes rise and flood over areas of north Queensland, the Northern Territory and northern Western Australia. Waterbirds, fish and other water animals breed in great numbers.

During the dry season, the moist air moves away, leaving fine, cooler, dry weather. The land dries out because there is no rain. Water levels in lakes and rivers drop and some dry out due to increased evaporation.

Subtropical climate

Most of the east coast of Australia, from Sydney in New South Wales to Townsville in Queensland, has a subtropical climate. Rain falls in the hot and humid summer months. Winter months are drier and cooler.

Temperate climate

South-east Victoria, Tasmania, the Australian Capital Territory and southern New South Wales have a temperate climate. Summers are warm and winters are cool. There is rain over the whole year.

A thunderstorm forms in the summer off Darwin, Northern Territory, bringing heavy rain.

Rainforest on Lord Howe Island, New South Wales, which is subtropical.

Temperate forests grow in Tasmania.

The Tasmanian highlands
have an alpine climate.

Alpine climate

The mountainous areas of Victoria, New South Wales and Tasmania have
an alpine climate. High in the mountains, air is cooler than on lower land.
In winter the air is cold enough for rain to freeze and fall as snow. Snow and
ice begin to melt when warmer weather arrives in spring. Melted water runs
off mountains and feeds into streams and rivers. It is an important source of
natural water for rivers such as the Murray and Snowy Rivers.

Mediterranean climate

Southern parts of Western Australia and parts of South Australia near Adelaide
have a Mediterranean climate. A Mediterranean climate has hot, dry summers
with little rain and high evaporation rates. In winter, temperatures are mild
and there is plenty of rain.

Bushland in Mediterranean
areas of South Australia can
cope with little rain.

Arid and semi-arid climate

Most of Australia's interior has an **arid** or semi-arid climate. Arid regions are very dry. Semi-arid regions get slightly higher rainfall as they are closer to the coast. Winds lose their moisture further inland, so arid regions are dry and sunny all year round. In summer, temperatures are often extremely hot. In winter, temperatures drop to below zero degrees Celsius on cloudless nights.

Rainbow Valley in the centre of Australia has an arid climate.

Yearly rainfall in six different climate types in Australia			
Location	**Climate**	**Average yearly rainfall**	**Wet months**
Darwin	tropical wet and dry	1659 mm	November–April
Brisbane	subtropical	1149 mm	mainly November–April
Melbourne	temperate	656 mm	any time of the year
Thredbo	alpine	1786 mm	rain any time of the year; snow in winter
Perth	Mediterranean	869 mm	June–August
Alice Springs	arid	279 mm	rare, but any time of year

Extremes in weather

The weather pattern in any region is sometimes interrupted by extremes in weather. Extreme weather affects the amount of water available for us to use, and the quality of that water. The most common extreme weather events in Australia are **droughts** and floods. Other extreme types of weather are cyclones and severe thunderstorms, which can cause destructive winds, hail and **torrential** rains.

Droughts

Droughts occur when less rainfall than average falls in a region. Waterways may dry up and plants die if a drought continues over a long period. Animals, such as kangaroos, may have difficulty finding enough natural water to drink and plants to eat.

Lack of rain during a long drought can kill crops, such as wheat. Livestock, such as sheep and cattle, die if they cannot find enough water to drink and their pastures have dried up. People living in cities and towns are affected by droughts when they have to follow water restrictions.

Land affected by drought in outback Western Australia is dry and cracked.

Waterwise Fact

Droughts in Australia

Australia has experienced severe droughts in 2001–05, 1982–83, 1946–47, 1895–1903. In the most recent drought, many crops failed and livestock died.

Markers on the road warn motorists how deep flood waters can get.

Floods

Floods happen when too much rain falls for the natural water systems to absorb. Flood waters pollute our waterways with rubbish and mud, and this can affect our water supply.

There are two types of flooding. Flash floods occur when very heavy rain falls in a short time. This sort of flooding can happen rapidly, causing deaths and damaging property. The second type of flooding happens when steady rain falls over longer periods. Rivers gradually fill to a point where they overflow, allowing water to spread over land into towns, cities and farmlands. Flooding of this type is usually more gradual, allowing people and animals time to move to safety. Some of this flooding is normal, such as during the summer months in northern Australia.

Waterwise Fact

Land clearing

Roots of trees and vegetation help hold the soil together and slow down the rate of run-off when it rains heavily. This reduces damage to the land. Clearing hilly land of its vegetation can make flooding more severe.

23

Cyclones and thunderstorms

Cyclones are huge storms that develop in tropical regions of the world. Cyclones are also known as hurricanes and typhoons.

Cyclones form over the ocean where the water temperature is above 26°C. These conditions exist in seas off north Queensland, the Northern Territory and north Western Australia. Water vapour rises out of a warm sea and causes winds to spin. Moisture and heat come together to form huge rain clouds and very strong winds. Heavy rain and winds of up to 300 kilometres per hour cause severe damage to life and property. The rain can cause flooding. Floodwater sweeps rubbish, mud and pollutants into the waterways, contaminating the natural water.

Thunderstorms can bring hail, flash flooding from torrential rain and destructive winds. Flash flooding also pollutes our waterways.

A thunderstorm can be seen approaching near Kalgoorlie, Western Australia.

Waterwise Fact

Cyclones

In 2005 Cyclone Ingrid travelled through Queensland, the Northern Territory and Western Australia. This grade five cyclone destroyed houses with 300-kilometre-per-hour winds and caused serious flooding. Some communities lost their supply of drinking water.

Drought is more common in Australia during an El Niño period.

El Niño

El Niño is a change in climate in the Pacific Ocean. In countries such as Australia, it causes less rainfall than normal.

El Niño occurs when a cold water mass that normally circulates in the Pacific Ocean off South America weakens. Warm water comes in and replaces the cold water. The cold water is forced across to the west where the water is normally warm. The cold water produces less water vapour, so there is less rainfall. The result is often severe drought, especially in eastern Australia.

El Niño caused a severe drought in South Australia and Victoria in the summer of 1982–83. The drought led to bushfires which killed many people.

The effects of El Niño can vary. South American countries get much higher than average rainfall because of the warm water mass off the coast.

Waterwise Fact

How often does El Niño happen?

On average, El Niño happens every two to seven years. The extreme weather varies, depending on how strong El Niño is.

Greenhouse gases

Greenhouse gases are gases in the Earth's atmosphere, such as carbon dioxide, that trap the Sun's heat and prevent some of the heat from escaping back into space. These gases help to keep the Earth's temperatures at a level where people, plants and animals thrive.

However, with our factories, motor vehicles and the burning of **fossil fuels**, we are producing more greenhouse gases every year.

Global warming

Global warming is the increase in the Earth's temperature all over the world. Many scientists believe the increase in greenhouse gases is making the global climate warmer. This will have a serious effect on our water.

Car traffic produces greenhouse gases.

Waterwise Fact

Methane gas

Methane is a greenhouse gas which is 25 times more effective at trapping heat than carbon dioxide. The average cow burps 500 litres of methane a day.

Waste products from this lead smelter produce greenhouse gases.

Low-lying islands such as these in the Caribbean may be covered by the sea due to global warming.

Water in a warmer world

As the Earth's temperature rises, icecaps and glaciers will melt. This will raise the sea levels, and some low-lying islands and coastal areas could become permanently flooded. All of this could change the climate.

Floods and droughts will happen more often. This will affect rainfall and run-off, so our supply of ground water will decrease.

Southern Australia may become drier with less rainfall and longer droughts. This could lead to food shortages because farmers will have no water for crops or livestock. If the oceans become warmer, cyclones in tropical regions could become stronger and more dangerous.

Murray–Darling River System

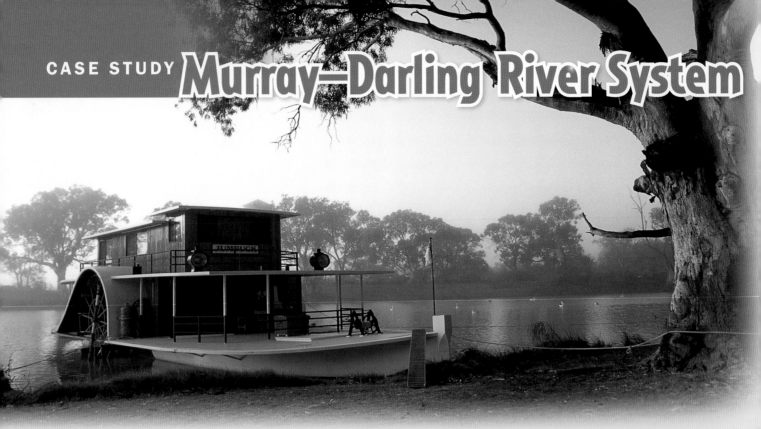

Paddle steamers were the main form of transport on the Murray–Darling River in the 1890s.

The Murray–Darling River System is the biggest river system and source of natural water in Australia. It is made up of two rivers, the Murray and the Darling, which come together in New South Wales. The total length of the two rivers is 3370 kilometres. The water in the rivers comes from New South Wales, Victoria, Queensland and South Australia. The Murray–Darling provides a home for many species of plants and animals, including the Murray cod, Australia's biggest freshwater fish.

Human impact

Scientists believe that Aboriginal people settled along the banks of the two rivers 40 000 years ago. They used the rivers for water, they fished for food and the riverbank trees provided wood for making canoes.

Later, early European settlers used the rivers for water, **irrigation**, fishing and transporting goods, such as wool, wood and crops. Towns along the rivers, such as Goolwa and Wentworth, became busy ports.

The Murray River winds across the land, supplying water to the plains.

Many river gums have died because of the high salt content in the water and the low water levels.

Problems and solutions

Today, most of the Murray–Darling River System is used for irrigating crops and supplying drinking water for Adelaide and other towns. Modern changes in agriculture and other industries are putting more pressure on this fragile river system.

More irrigation and recent droughts have meant that less water is entering the river system. This leaves less water for fish and other water animals and plants in the river.

Irrigation raises the water table and brings salt closer to the surface. The irrigation water flows through crops and soil then back into the river, bringing salt with it and making the river water increasingly salty. Too much salt is harmful to wildlife and makes the water undrinkable.

Planting trees and making irrigation more efficient, so less water is needed, can help reduce saltiness.

A wall controls flooding on the Murray–Darling River in Goolwa, South Australia.

Water forecast

Water is moving in a continuous cycle in nature. We depend on water to live but our lives also have an impact on the water cycle. People, animals and plants are linked to the water cycle and what we do will affect the water we have in the future.

If we conserve water, there will be more water to use in the future, our natural water will be healthier and the future quality and supply will be protected.

Protect and conserve water for our future.

Glossary

algal blooms	slime that covers the surface of water, caused by tiny plants called algae
aquifers	underground materials (such as rock or sand) containing a supply of water
arid	dry
atmosphere	the air around the Earth
bore	pipes and a pumping system that brings ground water to the surface
condensation	the process of water vapour changing into liquid water
droughts	long spells of below average rainfall
evaporates	changes from liquid water into water vapour through heat
fossil fuels	coal, oil and natural gas
glaciers	frozen rivers of ice
ground water	water found underground
industrial waste	rubbish that is left over after making products
irrigation	a system of channelling water to crops or livestock
porous	lets liquid pass through
precipitation	water falling as rain, hail or snow
run-off	water that flows down mountains, streets or across land
sewage	toilet waste
torrential	huge fall of rain
tributaries	rivers or streams flowing into a bigger river
water vapour	water in a gas form, such as steam or mist
wetlands	lakes, rivers and swamps

Index